praise for if you cannot find her

I love that this woman put all her emotions in this book. What a loving heart she has. I can totally relate to her words; I can totally feel her pains and her joys. This book is a gem. You will not regret purchasing it. When you reach the end, you are left satisfied but looking forward to experiencing more of her beautiful words…

MICHELLE B.

A beautiful collection of heartfelt poetry. It's such a delicate book, presented with cute illustrations. A book to revisit time and again. Wholly recommended.

S. ANDREWS

Something we all need to read. Both emotional, and empowering.

V. WILLIAMS

it's always been you

it's always been you

A COLLECTION OF POETRY & PROSE

SHEE

Copyright © 2023 by Shee

All rights reserved.

No part of this book may be reproduced in any form or by any electronic or mechanical means, including information storage and retrieval systems, without written permission from the author, except for the use of brief quotations in a book review.

Cover layout design by: Shee

Cover art: www.pexels.com - Irina Iriser @iriser_k

Book format design by: Shee

Illustrations by: Shee

ISBN: 978-1-7340199-3-3

Imprint: Independently published

For information regarding permission or distribution, contact Shee at Shee.poetry@gmail.com.

My forever family
Andres, Jacob, Messiah, Aiden & May

Yes, I will be a writer and make you all live again in my words.

> CARLOS BULOSAN

foreword

They say that matter is constant. So, since the beginning of Earth's creation, we have been here. Maybe not in the forms we have now, but every particle and atom we are made up of has been here since day one. Only as humans are we fully aware of what it means to exist. So, I like to think that maybe when all of this is over, and I take my last breath, my true purpose will come to be. Maybe it will be as a rose, a wildflower, or the lapping waves at our future generation's feet. Whatever it will be, I will be. I will always be here, always. And, so will you. Remember that.

- Shee, 2023

A Message to the Reader:

In September 2019, I released my first collection of poetry. It's a year that holds a special place in my heart. I felt empowered, confident, and on top of the world. Everything seemed to align perfectly, with my book as the shining centerpiece. Then came 2020, and the pandemic changed everything. I must admit, I'm not a fan of rollercoasters, and these past few years have been just like one - a tumultuous ride with ups and downs.

After publishing my first collection, I had set a goal to publish the next book in April 2020, but it didn't materialize. Slowly, the goal seemed to slip away and ended up on the back burner. You'd think that with four years to put the book together, I'd know precisely what to say to you. However, I'm torn between saying too much or not enough.

Who I was in 2019 is no longer the same person I am today. I'm sure many of you have also experienced significant changes and, like me, felt like there was no choice in the matter. I've become a different version of myself, leading a different life, and this book reflects that transformation. It's more raw, painful, and symbolizes breaking free from my comfort zone. If you've read my first collection, I'm certain you'll notice the difference, and I hope you can appreciate it.

In the introduction of my first book, I shared my insecurities about publishing and the hesitation I felt during the process. That's likely why I played it safe. The pieces in my first book were mostly micro poems and weren't very revealing. I was afraid of being too exposed and showing my deepest wounds to the world. Since then, my writing style has evolved, just as my life has. I am so proud of many of the pieces in this book and hope you find a piece that may resonate with you. As much as I've enjoyed my writing journey, I don't foresee another poetry collection in the future because, like everything else in my life, my writing habits have transformed. I hope I'm wrong, and that there's a future with more books and even more growth.

Sadly, I hardly write anymore. Maybe it's because I'm afraid to confront the pain I've buried deep within to keep functioning as an individual, wife, and mother. Not writing feels foreign, despite having so much to say. Since my first book, I've lost people, some by choice, and some sadly to death. I also lost a part of myself in the process. Although I know I'll never be the same, I'm trying to find my way back to the empowered and confident parts of me. For a while, I wrote every day, pouring words onto paper like a release, much like exhaling. But now, writing has become more than therapy; it's like an extinguisher to a burning flame.

In this collection, there are still poems about the Moon (yes, I still love the Moon), but not as many. Like in "If You Cannot Find Her," there isn't a specific theme to this book. However, I must issue a warning: there are many pieces that touch on sensitive topics like abuse, death, attempted suicide, disordered eating, and more. Even as I read some of the pieces now, my chest tightens, and I worry about how you might perceive me. All I can say is that I'm grateful for my life, even though it's been filled with pain. I have a beautiful life, and the fact that I'm still trying to figure out who I am and who I'm trying to become, all while healing from trauma, is a blessing I don't take for granted. I hope you can still find happiness and pride within the pages of this book and appreciate the contradictions from one poem to the next. Like my first book, there are several interactive prompts included, and I hope they

INTRODUCTION

inspire you to write more and enhance your experience with this book.

Something new in this collection is the inclusion of my artwork, which I didn't do in my first one. I've always doodled since I was a child, and in my journals, you'd find sketches related to whatever I was writing about. Most of what I've included here are drawings of plants. I'm undeniably a plant enthusiast, or as I like to say, a plant mom. I hope you enjoy these drawings as much as I enjoyed creating them.

Some of my writing is open to interpretation, while other pieces reflect my experiences. I'll let you decide which are which. Many encapsulate not only my own struggles but those of others as well. I've even included a couple of journal entries, a last-minute decision, making it even more personal. I ask that you read with an open heart and avoid judging what you may not fully understand. We all interpret things differently, and much of what I've written may or may not resonate with your life. You might relate to some pieces or not. Perhaps you'll know someone who needs to read a particular piece. If so, I encourage you to share it with them.

I dedicate this book to my husband and children, and my loving friends and family. However I'd like to specifically name a few who inspired so much of the poetry within this book. To my father, whom I hadn't seen or spoken to for eight years before his passing, I'm grateful to have found understanding between us before he left Earth-side. Many of my poems are about my father, but two in this book have a different tone. His illness was ironic because it brought us together, but it also quickly took him away as he passed less than three months after his diagnosis. There is still pain in our past, but as we laid him to rest, I also laid to rest much of my resentment towards

INTRODUCTION

him. Setting aside those feelings has made my love for him grow. Even though our relationship was fractured, I wouldn't want to change a thing because I accept that our lives played out as they were meant to be. Rest easy, Dad.

I also want to dedicate this book to my bestie, Cindy Lou. I'm not sure how I would have gotten through these years without her. I'm thankful the Universe brought us together exactly around the time we needed each other most. In 2020, when everything was in upheaval, Cynthia experienced a loss no mother should ever have to endure. Her daughter, my little bestie, passed away due to surgical complications a few months before her second birthday. That little angel left a lasting impression on me and anyone who ever met her. She was beautiful, silly, and her laughter and giggle, simply infectious. This year she would have been five. There's not a day that I don't think of her. Every time I see a butterfly, I know with the depth of me, it's her stopping by to say hello. You will find a few poems in this book for Yaretzi. This book is for her too, so she will forever be remembered, long after we are all gone.

A few short months after my father passed, my oldest sister suddenly became ill. The situation was touch and go, and I had no idea if she was going to make it. There are so many tender parts to her story, and my heart aches thinking about the situation and how her illness is affecting her family. I am grateful every day that my sister is still here, but she is no longer who she once was. A day changed everything. And although her heart still beats, I mourn our relationship, and I mourn her. There have been many times in our lives together when our relationship was complicated, many periods when we had no contact. I know everything happens for a reason, but if I could, I would go back and hug my sister tighter each time we said goodbye or stayed on the phone a little longer when she missed me and just wanted to check in. No one will ever understand how our childhood impacted us both, how alone we often felt, and how we had to rely on each other to find the strength to get through our days. She was my protector, and I miss her. I miss her loud mouth, her funny laugh, and all the little things she did to make sure I knew she loved me. There are pieces for and about my sister that I hope one day I can share with her.

Above all, this book is for all of you. I want to express my deepest gratitude for your support. Thank you for choosing to embrace this part of my life and my heart.

With love, always,
Shee

SHEE

We tell ourselves that loving hard is a super power
Yet all I've ever felt when it comes to love is powerless
Because we all know
Whoever loves less in a relationship
Holds all the power
And here I've always been
A prisoner of my own love
Begging for a chance to be set free

It was loud before
Deafening even
The way our hands screamed for a forever
Now, the hands hold in silence
A sign we should let go
But, even in the raucous of our demise
We can't let go
Baby, will you let me go?
Please (don't) let (me) go

Sometimes the way the hands hold (or do not) tells us more than we think…

SHEE

Clink, clink, clink
Clink, clink, clink
One of my favorite sounds, in the world
Is the way the spoon sounds in a mug
Hitting the sides, almost on purpose
Like music for refreshed ears
My heart believes in its pure magic

Clink, clink, clink
Clink, clink, clink
As it performs a ceremony
Of mixing cream and liquid gold
It always takes me back to when I was four
Rubbing the sleep from my almond-shaped eyes
Pushing back the nightmares that invaded my slumber
Only to hear the clinking of my Mother's spoon

Stirring ever so gently, as she poured her hazelnut creamer
Into the dark abyss of her magical Arabica juice
Soon after, the smell reached my room
Prompting me to rise
I got out of bed slowly
Dragging my feet
Black Bear in tow *(oh, how I miss you)*

Contemplating how I'd muster the courage
To ask her for some
Peeking from the entrance to the kitchen
Her back facing me
Rolling her change, a weekend routine
She always seemed to enjoy
Mommy?
She spun in her seat towards me
…

Her smile reaching her eyes first
Somehow already knowing I'd ask
She poured me creamer with a dash of coffee

Clink, clink, clink
Clink, clink, clink
And, we sat there, enjoying our coffee
As she rolled her coins, and me, savoring the moment
Wishing it would last forever
Safe in the moment where no monsters could hurt me
Fictional or real

Safe in a moment just her and I

Clink, clink, clink
Clink, clink, clink

What does healing look like?

A list…
- a flick of a match
That lights your favorite candle

- the steam from the water
As you draw a bubble bath

- the mist from a spray bottle
As you water your favorite plant

- the prickling of damp grass
As you watch the clouds go by

- the paint on your hands
As you create another piece of art

- the mud on your boots
From your hike to see the sunrise

… unfinished & unending

Write a list of what healing looks like for you below.
Also, cheers to healing and cheers to you.

*

*

*

*

*

*

*

*

*

*

*

*

SHEE

In the beginning…
I fell so deeply for him
It was him, only him
The way he smiled with his eyes
And the way he laughed with his heart
The way he made me feel safe in nothing but his arms
How I could only breathe if he was near
How nothing was worth celebrating unless it was with him
How my world was meant to be shared with his
And how I wanted everything to be us
Even if that meant I was no longer me

But as time went on
I fell so deeply because of him
It was him, it was always him
The way he smiled with lies in his eyes
And the way he laughed without any heart
The way he made me feel unsafe in nothing but his arms
How I could never breathe if he was near
How nothing was worth celebrating unless he said it was
How my world wasn't meant to be shared with his
And how I wanted everything not to be us
Even if that meant I was no longer me

But, then…
He fell so deeply because of me
He noticed I was no longer me
Because he was no longer him
The way I no longer looked him in the eyes
And the way I hurt his heart
When I ignored his laughter
The way he tried to make me feel safe again
But I no longer looked for security in his arms
…

How he could never breathe unless I was near
How nothing was worth his celebration
Unless it was with me
How he wanted nothing but to share our worlds
And how he wanted everything to be us, again
But I was no longer her
He tried, but it was too late
I was no longer her

To all the women who are no longer her…

To all the tomorrows
That may never come
I love you most

I love you most!

IT'S ALWAYS BEEN YOU

Darkness bleeds heart first
Feathered leaves and crimson blood
Life and death, the same

Write a haiku using the word **darkness** below:

A haiku is 3 lines. The first line is 5 syllables,
the second is 7 syllables, and the last line is 5 syllables.

SHEE

I didn't learn
I stepped into the fire
Expecting rain
Was burned, but smiled anyway
The smoke swirled into my airways
And hugged my lungs
It was a comforting pain
Knowing it could take me if it wanted to
But played with me instead

Don't lie…
    I know you play with fire, too.

And maybe I have never felt good enough
Because no one ever showed me I was

SHEE

It's hard to admit
But yes, I have wanted to die
Many times in this life of mine
But more often than that
I have wanted nothing more than to live
Call it what you want
Baby, I call that a win

It breathes
In the mundane
In rage
In silence
Even atop the blades
Of dewy morning grass
Poetry lives

SHEE

> I know I once said I'd wait for you anywhere
> But one life is all you get to break me
> You won't find me in the next lifetime
> *I promise — I swear*
> You will never find me there

I sit in the violence of missing you
Trying to find comfort in the rage of grief
Hating with every cell of me
The disease that robbed you of your freedom
That swindled you out of an identity that was once yours
The one built by experience, trauma, laughter, and love

The disease that took future memories
I had hoped we would share
That took the arguments we will never find resolution for
Now I have no choice but to succumb
To the type of mourning
As though missing you were not enough
That only exists when it is for someone
Whose heart still beats

Holding sharp breaths
While praying you continue to take yours
Anxiety now forever taking up space
Within the chambers of my heart
Fearing that I never will get you back
Maybe fear is knowing but with a hint of hope
Saying your name in whispers
Like a prayer to bring you back

Come back to me…
Please, come back

SHEE

You broke me under the skin
Like a bruise, but no rainbow of colors
You damaged what I once believed
To be my strongest muscle—
This heart, so injured
It now beats with hesitation

But, unlike bruises
This heart may never heal
So, I cover it up
With layers of smiles and insincere positivity
Concealing the truth, like a secret I wish to tell
But cannot
Because hearts can't talk
And these lips are sealed

Maybe the way they loved you
Was their best
Was all they knew how to show
Was everything they had to give
But, even then...
That doesn't mean you have to accept it
Even then, you get to control how you share yourself

                               Even then, it's okay to walk away...

SHEE

She lights the candle
Champagne-colored
With a faint scent of peach
She sits cross-legged
On the cold, hard floor
Regretting her choice of shorts
But letting the chill wake her
Afraid of the fire
But somehow, in love with the flame

She watches as it dances
A show she's privileged to see
It's been a tough year
But beautiful too
Troubling circumstances
But joyous memories too
She's lost some people
But found home in some too
It's been what it was meant to be
And it was, what it was, when it needed to be
And she's grateful, even if it nearly killed her

Closed eyes, no wishes
Only letting those feelings hit her one last time
Then a deep inhale
Goodbye can feel good, I promise
And she blows out the candle
Opens her eyes, sees the smoke and knows
We must close finished chapters
To begin new ones

IT'S ALWAYS BEEN YOU

SHEE

Wait for him in the garden
Of a million dying promises
That you overwater with salted tears

When he arrives, crawl to him
Just as he likes

Lift him and his burdens
Atop your weak shoulders
And carry them as your own

Bathe him in sweet lavender
And dress his wounds
As he rips open yours

Use your days to prepare his favorite meals
But, always eat alone

Bend over backwards to please him
While he sits upon your chest
Informing you, it's still not good enough

Caress his broken
As he pokes around at yours

Allow your ears to bleed
As he reminds you of your flaws

Swallow your opinions
Because he is always right

Keep waiting
…

Because his time is his own
And he has no time for you

Hold his slippery hand
And don't ask him for his forever

Accept the apologies
He is never willing to give

Love him, but lose yourself

SHEE

I remember when I saw those two blue lines
On the little white and pink stick
That your Daddy bought and could barely afford

Sixteen and seventeen
A couple of kids
So in love with possibility
But not yet ready for responsibility

I cried
Maybe because I was scared
But I think because somehow I felt whole
For once I would experience a love
That cost more physically
Then it ever would emotionally

Because everything you have ever given me
Giggles
Tantrums
Years
Has always been a gift that I will never deserve
A treasure I can never repay

They called me
A statistic
A good for nothing
A whore

They called you
A bastard
That poor child
A son of a bitch

…

IT'S ALWAYS BEEN YOU

But it has never been my intention
To prove anything to them
But to you instead

Because even if I am your Mother
We have grown up together
Watched each other stumble and fall

We've held each other on hard nights
And laughed when the day came around

You, you are my first true love
My greatest motivator
The love that exceeds my worth

Yet, here we are striving
Here we are surviving
Together

And anything I've never received
Wasn't meant for me

But, Son…
You have always been mine
And, look what magic you've become

So much of what I've needed to say
Has been said in the rhythm of an exhale

Reminder: *B R E A T H E*

Sometimes, when no one is looking
I disappear to play a game
Of *hide and seek* with Insecurity

On the days when she doesn't want to play
She finds me quickly
And, it's rather boring then

Other times, when she wants a bit of fun
She will sneak off to my home as I hide
To sleep in my bed
And mess up my sheets

She will read my journals
And write discouraging notes

Sing my favorite Whitney songs
And then delete them from my playlist

Kiss my children on the forehead
But forget to pack them lunch

And even dance in the forbidden garden
Mine and my husband's favorite nighttime ritual

All the while, allowing me to believe I'm good at hiding
But in reality, she's so good at being me

Oh, Insecurity...

Stop moving mountains
For people who are too afraid to climb them

you're so not helping…

Tell me, what do you daydream of?
(Write it below)

I do not expect anything of you
That is not within you in the first place
I do not seek to change who you are
For that responsibility is all yours

So, if your vibes are off
If I feel your intentions are inauthentic
If you intend to use me
Or the people I love
I will feel it
And, in turn
I will delete your permanence from my life

The mere memory of you will fade
Into the abyss that is the past

I will not make myself available
To those who damage what doesn't belong to them

Love,

_____

(Sign your name)

I hope there comes a day
Where you wake up
And love *(for yourself)*
Greets you with open arms

SHEE

In the dusty, sometimes forgotten attic
That lives within my heart
I keep a memory of us
I sneak up there from time to time
Usually when sleep eludes me

On those nights I climb the creaky ladder
Swat the cobwebs
That search for solace on my face
And I search for that memory
I always forget where I put it
Until I see the box labeled, *Once Upon A time*

But when I do, there it is
A brief view of what we were
What we never continued to be
It is one of very few memories we have together
Where we laugh
And where I still call you *Daddy*

We are driving in your old truck
Black, I think
And I can barely see over the dash
I have no idea where we are going
But it wouldn't matter
Because I don't remember anything past the laughter

I don't remember if we were traveling towards excitement
Or maybe, towards disappointment
I don't know my age
Or what I was wearing
The color of the day
Or if it was real
…

Did I create this memory?
Was it a dream?
Does it matter?
It's here

This fragile memory
Between the beats and pumps
Of this broken heart
Its home, my heart
Where even the things that have broken me live

SHEE

He laughs as he spills the gas he will soon light
But you just stand there
Knowing what will happen
What always happens

You brace yourself for the roar of flames
That you've come to know by name
It hurts
It burns
An excruciating sting
An agony you're all to familiar with

When he's done admiring the beauty of the flame
He will put the fire out slowly
And blame you for making him light it

He is blinded by power
But must not know what he is creating
Because nothing soft comes from flames

Like a Phoenix, she will rise

What is your greatest fear? Why?
(Write it below)

SHEE

> What if this was your last storm?
> Wouldn't it be worth holding on
> To see the Sun rise just for you…

I sit and stare at the Moon
It is all of itself
Full and bright
Blessing the night
With its blooming confidence
I heard once that the Sun and Moon were lovers
But maybe once they were Father and Daughter
I sit and stare
I sit…
I cry
I ask…
I beg
Tell me, Mr. Moon
How does one let go
When they've barely found the courage
To hold on

ACR
1963-2022

SHEE

I was only six
Sitting at the round wooden table
In the kitchen with the ugly carpet
At the house in the hills
Where you force fed me
What I could never swallow willingly

It was always me
The last one at the table
Hating myself for getting too full, too fast
Envying my siblings who were all finished
Forgetting all about me
As they ran outside to play

I wanted to make you happy
And eat the fucking food
But my mouth and my stomach
Would not cooperate
You knew I hated onions
Probably the same way you hated me
But, you served them to me anyway

Throwing up on my plate
Made you furious
As you scraped the vomit to the side
Only to scoop up more cabbage and onions
To violently feed me
Hitting the spoon against my teeth
I closed my eyes
Wishing the moment were only a bad dream

I felt so alone then
Like the loneliness I feel now
…

IT'S ALWAYS BEEN YOU

Unable to tell anyone
About these feelings that still plague me
Shame feels like loose change in my pocket
Heavy, but still worth something I'm sure
Maybe that is when it started
This complicated relationship with food

The years of…
The bingeing
The purging
The recovery
The relapse

I look into the mirror with blood shot eyes
Crying as quietly as possible
So my daughter doesn't hear me in the other room
Flushing the toilet
Like it is full of misplaced dreams

SHEE

Mom, did I get anything from you?
She asks, as I'm brushing her long brown hair
What do you mean?
Unsure of where the conversation is headed

Like your laugh? Or your toes?
I giggle at her curiosity
And start to twirl her hair in my fingers
To distract myself from the pain
As it lurks its way to my chest

Go play now, Love...
Doing my best to disguise the cracking in my voice
As she leaves, I reach out but let her go and play

I want to tell her the truth
I want to explain
That daughters inherit the scars of their mothers
And, that her inheritance is anything but wealth
Instead, she was gifted a heavy burden
That I never wished for her

I want to tell her that when she cries, she sheds my tears
And, that her anger was given to her
Long before she was ever born
That in the future she will look for love
In all the wrong places
When she only need to look within herself

But, she's seven
And, this is a conversation for when she's older
Instead, I will continue to plant gardens around her scars
...

To uplift and contribute to her growth
So, maybe one day she will understand
Beauty can come from pain

She is my proof of this, and her daughter will be hers

What a privilege it is to see the happiness in others
Even if you often wish the happiness was yours

I won't tell if you don't

It wasn't the years
You didn't call that made me sad
It was the years you did
The ones where you offered hope as a gift
Always accented with a promise
All pretty like a sparkly bow

The years you didn't call
Were always a welcomed relief
No tug-o-war of emotion within my brittle chest
No guilt for not believing your words were gold
No ice from these hands that were searching for warmth

But each year I kept my own traditions
Of wishlists and melancholic song writing
I knew from a young age Santa didn't exist
And I was sure that if he did
His gifts wouldn't extend to little brown bastards
With too optimistic a heart

But, I wrote him letters just in case
And tucked them beneath my mattress
Along with the daddy-issue-filled songs

And each year it was the same
I wished you'd have a Merry Christmas
Even if you didn't share it with me

SHEE

That is the thing about people
The ones you love most
The ones you lose sleep over
The ones you (feel you) need

They change
And there's nothing you can do about it
But watch the transformation of someone you once knew

You will be faced with an inevitable choice
You either deal
Or walk away

The choice may never be easy
But, the choice is yours

Teach me, Mr. Moon
Teach me to acquiesce
The sadness within my solitude
Illuminate my heart
And allow me to cozy up to
Desolation and despair

I have so much to learn...

SHEE

You played this song
A sweet song for everyone to hear
And, they loved it…they loved you
But I always heard beyond what you were playing

I heard your song for what it was
A plagiarized style, with auto-tuned creativity
Yet, I listened and appreciated it anyway
I listened because everyone deserves a chance to be heard

I listened because I believed if I listened long enough
I would eventually hear the same song
Everyone else heard
But your subliminals were too loud for me to ignore

It's sad, really, this person you claim to be
Who's not even close to who you are
You connivingly overshadow insincerity in your song
With a faux melody

But, I hear it (*I can't un-hear it*)
I can't make others hear what I hear so loudly
And it isn't my place to tell them of your false empathy

But, it's okay
One day they will understand
Why I no longer listen to your song
And, truth be told

I don't much fancy, one-hit wonders

IT'S ALWAYS BEEN YOU

SHEE

There's a picture of us
Just us three
A sweet moment in time
A memory only illuminated by the printing of paper
You, me, and mommy
The Three Musketeers
As I would often call us

But usually, it was you and I who held on together
In desperation
In fear
By necessity
But, I'd be silly not to recognize
That often, and with no choice, we fought alone

Who had it worse?
A comparison I won't be making
Because you became the first step
And I, mostly soft, chose to hide behind you

In the photo, your smile is so bright
Your eyes even brighter
I often think of the burden you carried
Being the oldest
The first "step" (child)
Me, the "second"

You have always been *my protector*
Haven't you?

In the photo my eyes are on you
My protector
For mommy was too in love
…

To see the darkness we inescapably faced
All those years
Just you and me
Me and you

Just us
Just us
Just us

A sweet moment in time
A rare occasion
Before your disease robbed you
Of living the life you so bravely fought to have
Before your disease robbed me of my protector

My sissy, my protector

SHEE

I don't want or need recognition
For the things I have lived through
As I sat, feeling helpless
Watching my world burn
The things that have caused me to dig my own grave
As I contemplated whether to blanket myself in dark Earth
The things that have ripped me open
As I clenched my own heart
Willing to give it to anyone who cared enough to hold it

No, I don't want recognition
I don't need a *bravo*
Or a pat on the back
No, no pity party for me
Because anything I have lived through
Need not be recognized by anyone other than me

I want to revel in them all on my own
I want to dance with flame
Plant gardens next to my grave
And, place my heart where it belongs
Always within myself

IT'S ALWAYS BEEN YOU

Things you have survived:

*

*

*

*

*

*

*

*

*

*

*

*

*

*

***Now, play your favorite celebration song on blast and dance! Revel in it, all on your own!

SHEE

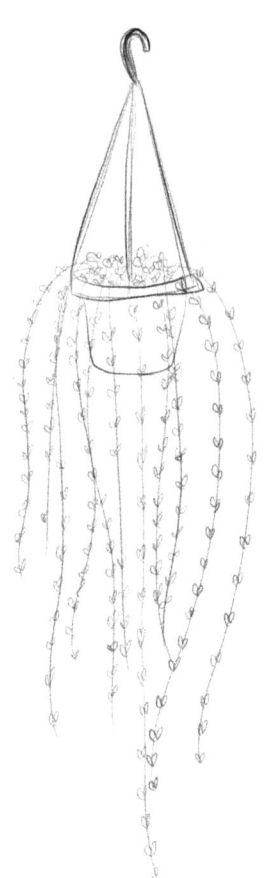

IT'S ALWAYS BEEN YOU

Who do you miss most in this world?
What would you tell them if you had the chance?
(Write them a letter below)

This is everything
This power of acceptance.

December 31, 2019, Day 365 of 365

What this past year has taught me is that the things we try to control are usually the ones that end up hurting us the most, especially when they don't go our way. It's not easy, but accepting what is, is powerful. To be able to look at yourself in the mirror and say,

"I've got this! It's okay! What is meant for me will be!"

...is an incredible feeling. Learning that I don't need to bend further than I have to is the peace I've been looking for and am only now perfecting. When it comes to relationships with significant others, friends, or family, you need to realize that the other person has their struggles too. They have pain, hurt, loss, stress, etc. So, even when a connection is severed, and it may be painful, try to accept it. Allow the disconnection to be a positive thing. Allow growth for both you and that individual. Be better because of the disruption. Know that everything has a purpose. Understand that maybe it wasn't you (or perhaps it wasn't them) that caused the rift...try to accept that maybe all the other issues that all of us have made it complicated.

So, although a loss may sound like a bad thing, in my opinion, it isn't. You always need to lose to appreciate the gain, but grow and be better because of it.

I kept on loving
But never myself
In all fairness
You kept taking
And never told me it was enough

So, I kept giving
Giving
And giving
Giving until I was all used up

To all the promises that never were
I waited for you, and it was a hopeful waiting
A longing, stitched behind the smile
Of an optimistic soul

I sat in cafes, sipping lukewarm coffee
Anxious to call you my friend
I wore my fancy dress coat
And strolled the vibrant city
Hoping you'd find your way
I took a little longer to step off the bus
Hoping you would greet me
But you never did

You were never meant to be mine
And I was never meant to be yours
Sometimes our desires lack fruition
Because they're not meant to touch
The surface of excitement and relief
But, I do wish it didn't hurt so bad

To all the promises that never were

i often feel the uncomfortable wave of loneliness
in such a crowded world
i am loved
but often last
i am strong
but often broken
i choose, most days
to continue my life as a person molded by fear
fear of not being chosen
…accepted
…acknowledged
…revered
oh, don't mind me
i do this a lot
but, i wish i would stop
o v e r t h i n k i n g

SHEE

The rain welcomed you
The day you were born
You, a gift from the heavens
A treasure I have never deserved
I never meant to be the mother
So terrified of affection
Rarely giving you softness
But mostly thorns instead

Our whole lives together
I've walked with shame
Holding its hand
Feeling less than a mother
And more of a depressed shell of woe

But, it never mattered, did it?
The adoration you've always had for me
The eagerness to make me proud
I know how it has often seemed
Like nothing could ever be good enough

But, I promise, *I declare*
That all I have ever hoped for in life
Lives in every breath you take
And I hope that one day you will understand
That the burden I have carried
The price all mothers pay
Is the act of becoming

Becoming…
Stronger
Wiser
A healed, healthier version of myself
…

IT'S ALWAYS BEEN YOU

While you've had to witness the
Tears
Mistakes
Failures

A burden I didn't know took part in raising you, too
An unfortunate consequence of having a mother
Cultivated by trauma
Carved by the sharp edges of loneliness

If I could have
I would have waited until the Sun was shining
To birth you into the world
So light greeted you instead
Of the pitter-patter of pain, falling from the sky

SHEE

I kept blaming the people who hurt me
Cursing them for the walls built around my heart
But I was wrong
It was never them who constructed those barriers
It was me
They just handed me the tools

And, I used them quite well...

There's a world on fire
A Phoenix rising, she is
Bring all of the flames

Write a haiku, using *fire* below:

Often we are stuck looking up towards the heavens
Searching for answers
Praying for a miracle
Begging for forgiveness
To a God we need
To a God we want
When we need them to be
What we want them to be
Sometimes...
God is right in front of us

Waiting for us to look down

Here I am, once more
In this foggy space of uncertainty
I dance around so gracefully here
Like I've rehearsed for years
No flowers grow here
Only weeds of self-doubt
No sun shines here
Only glimmers of a hopeful heart
Even the Moon's glow can't be seen
Only the dull sparkle of these tired eyes
This place has always been mine
But I've never wanted to know it
To be here is to be lost

Here I am, again
In this foggy space of uncertainty
And I can't remember how to get out
There's no choice but to dance
So, I dance

SHEE

March 16, 2020
Day 1, Self-Isolation

It is morning, 10:09 to be exact
Woken by the sunlight peeking through the blinds
I am reminded that the light will always find its way
Even during the darkest of days
Everyone is still deep in slumber
Even the silly dog can't seem to wake
But here I am, awake
Instead of rising to make a cup of coffee
I lay in bed
Feeling everything
All the things I've been running from
Are finally catching up to me
I close my eyes and rub my face
I'm scared
Anxiety, turned to high
Depression, not too far behind
The pressure I always manage to bury deep
Is looking for a way to escape
I see it in the way my hands tremble
And the way I trip over my own feet

We are all supposed to be awake
All of us
Doing chores
Homework
Activities
Inside this home
The one they say we shouldn't leave
It should be bustling
Like the streets of our favorite city
…

But, it's not
There is no motivation to rise
Only to sleep the days away
Praying this is over before we know it
But knowing not to get our hopes up

Everyone is still sleeping
And it's okay
I will feel everything
Just so they don't need to

SHEE

The air smells here, like oil and onions
I hate onions
It is thick and pungent
Making it hard to breathe
And it is hot, just like all the summers before
I am sitting in my pink polka dot shorts
My favorite piece of clothing
That I should have retired months ago
Sitting cross-legged on a splintery wooden chair
I force the tears to stay in
And it is making my chest burn
After being told I have the feet of a monkey
And that I smelled like one too

The truth is I'd rather be in hell
Than have to sit in the company
Of this woman
The one who is about five tones lighter than me
The one who birthed the father
Who isn't biologically mine
The one who told my mother
That English is the language of America
And there is no room for foreign tongues

The one who force-fed me
A vile concoction of cabbage and onions
Did I mention I hate onions?
At the time, I imagined it was my favorite Filipino dish
Just to hold back more vomit
In the kitchen of my childhood home
A home that was filled with steps but no stairs
A home where I felt embarrassed to be seen
…

Because if she could not love my skin
If she could not love my being
How could I love me?
How could I be me?

DROWN ME IN MISTAKES
BURY ME IN DEPRESSION
I WILL STILL SURVIVE...

I held you in my hand once
And you fit so perfectly
Tucked safely in my sweaty palm
So gentle and warm
How stupid of me to let you go
As quick as I had found you...

Hope.

SHEE

On a Summer day that weakens me from the brutal heat
I step out of my skin
Allowing my scars a chance to breathe
I tiptoe in front of the mirror
And admire the roadmap of scars
Contributed so carelessly by my step-grandmother
My fingers trace the scars, each with its own story
Some weirdly tender after all this time
And I pause at the one beneath my breast
The one closest to my heart
A memory etched so vividly in my mind

I was eight years old, when she sat me on my twin bed
Punishing me with her words
As if I hadn't already been wounded enough
In a home filled with thorn-filled steps but no stairs
Trying her best to fill me with her lies and propaganda
Telling me all the sexual abuse I had endured
Was merely a product of childhood imagination
A seed planted in my head by my big sister
The one person who I knew loved me more than the world
But, who knew nothing of what had happened to me

I sat nodding, wanting to scream
A part of me yearning to believe her words
Wishing they were the truth so I wouldn't feel so damaged
But deep down, I knew I would only come to resent her
For the lies she attempted to drape me in
Was she trying to help?
Perhaps
Or maybe she was trying to alleviate the guilt she felt
Knowing she had recklessly exposed my innocence
To the hands of a man who would change my life forever
…

But, maybe doesn't matter
It doesn't matter!
It can't change the past
It couldn't then, and it can't now
Maybe doesn't erase the fact
That I still feel the anchor of his touch
As I drift into sleep some nights
I didn't blame her then, the way I do now
Because then I so badly wanted to be loved by her
I was blinded by my need for her love and acceptance
Hindered by my hope that she might one day care for me

Back then, I was innocent, soft, and bruised
Unaware that not all love was meant for me
Maybe she didn't have the capacity to love me
But had she, it is irrelevant now
Because I have learned
That her affection was no good for me

All I wanted was help, understanding
But most of all, I longed to be held
And told I wasn't broken goods
She had the power to help me
To hold my hands, offering reassurance
That none of it was my fault
She could have explained that at eight years old
I couldn't possibly be pregnant
Which I mistakenly believed

Something I was sure happened
When a man touched a woman
In the ways he had touched me
She could have told me
…

SHEE

That it took nine months to birth a child

And not the three years I had been waiting for
She could have educated me on what menstruation was
And its significance in the creation of life
She could have told me…
She could have told me
It was okay to look a man in the eyes
Without fear of his touch when no one was looking
And that one day, a man would love me
Making the scars he left behind feel magical

But she will never get that chance
And I will always have this scar

IT'S ALWAYS BEEN YOU

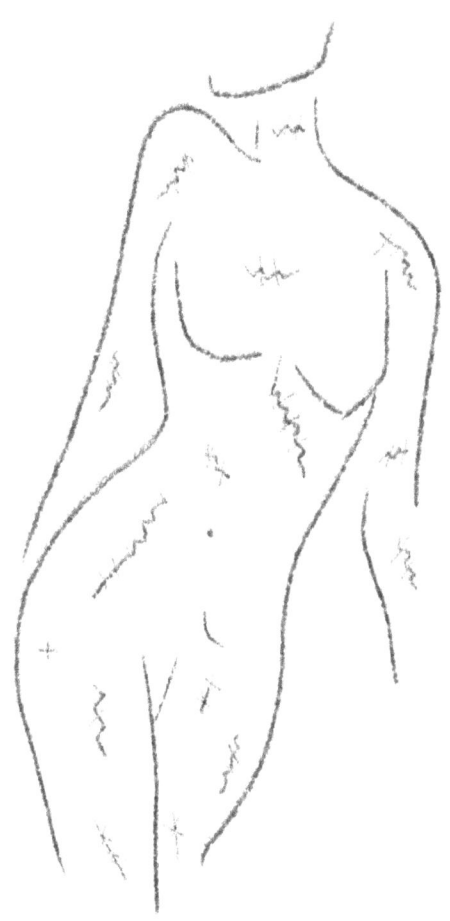

SHEE

On the days she wears her smile just a bit longer
And where laughter becomes
Her primary mode of communication
On those days, those ones
That is when she feels beautiful

Baby, don't you know
Your heart still beats without them?

(Write a list of things that keep your heart beating)

*

*

*

*

*

*

*

*

*

SHEE

I lack the heart to tell the ocean
I swim in her waters
And, walk her solitary shores
Merely to feel the pull of the Moon
Or to admit to the meadows
I run through her blossoming, butterfly-filled fields
As the Sun sets
So I can welcome the Moon with song and dance

I'm not bold enough to reveal to the mountains
That I use their strength-filled forms
And their highest summits as stepping-stones
To be closer to the Moon
Knowing I'll never reach him
In the same way he evokes me
Knowing I am only a human
A human yearning to be the sky

Because it is the sky that cradles the Moon
And oh, what I'd do for a chance
To show the Moon how much he is loved

Vulgar fingers fight
Resistance from innocence
Screams of those who lose

Write a haiku, using ***resistance*** below:

October 11, 2019
Journal Entry 284 of 365

Some of us never learned how to love ourselves. We didn't grow up hearing that we are strong, worthy, and beautiful. Consequently, we often seek constant validation from others. We work tirelessly to gain their approval, as if shouting, "Hello, here I am!" We morph into altered versions of ourselves in an attempt to be more appealing. Yet, when these efforts fall short, we are left feeling angry, hurt, and resentful. We end up manifesting all the things we struggle to escape.

When you encounter people going through this, take them under your wing and love them. Love them even more when it's challenging. Be everything they aspire to be and show them a love that requires nothing in return. In doing so, you can become a symbol of change for them. Be the catalyst for transformation.

My name is _____

I am STRONG

I am WORTHY

I am BEAUTIFUL

I am _____

I am _____

I am _____

And, I will...

Be KIND

Be BRAVE

Be BOLD

I will be _____

I will be _____

I will be _____

SHEE

Talisay, a province in the Philippines,
Is where Mommy once called home
The place she grew up speaking *Ilongo* and *Tagalog*
And where she ran the dirt roads
Hand in hand with her twin sister Uno
They called Mommy Dos
Mommy was always kind
More than willing to help others
Even if she didn't have to
You'd find her hip to hip
Helping the family's domestics cook and clean
In the big house where Mommy was one of fifteen

I often imagine Mommy as a child
Wishing upon falling stars
Dreaming of what her life could be
A politician like my Lolo?
A pageant star like my Lola?
No, her dreams were set West
American opportunity boundless

Mommy moved to the States
With her first husband, the sailor
To chase her American dream
But after Mommy had sissy, husband one left
Later, sissy and Mommy moved in with my bio-dad
Big sissy was Uno
And I became Dos

Mommy and bio-dad's forever didn't last long
After Mommy met her next husband
We moved to East Side San Jose
Becoming more disconnected from her former self
…

As she did her best to prove her American-ness
In the home,
Where Mommy was belittled into speaking only English

Don't speak that, this is America
From the step-family
Who didn't like us much
But, Mommy got clever
She adapted to the hostility and negativity
Becoming accustomed to the customs of those
Who did not value Filipino tradition

In the middle of her hope-filled metamorphosis
To become all things American
There was me, who had no choice but to play along
Growing up, I never got to visit Talisay
Never met Mommy's twin sister Uno

I ate "American cuisine"
The soggy meatloaf, the Chicken a la King
I spoke the West Coast slang
Yes, I say *Hella*
And memorized the music
Like Fleetwood Mac & The Carpenters

But it didn't matter how much I tried
I just wasn't American enough
My skin, the color of caramel
That was left on the heat a little too long
But when I was lucky
I'd get to see a glimpse of Filipino culture
With treats like Lechon and pancit canton
Karaoke and mah-jong
…

But even with a belly full of food and laughter
The reminders of how disconnected I was
From my Filipino roots were everywhere
From the slaps on my hands
From bio-dad's family
Because I didn't know
Which hand held the spoon or the fork

Disapproving stares
When I shook the hands of elders
Instead of raising them to my forehead
As a sign of respect and blessing

And, although I didn't know the language
I could hear their tones
I just wasn't Filipino enough
I wanted to be accepted by both
Americans and Filipinos, but instead
I've always been torn between the two worlds
Holding onto both
With little more than hope and insecurity

You see, some people's dreams
Become another's nightmare

Mommy your dream is my nightmare

IT'S ALWAYS BEEN YOU

SHEE

If you are asked to cross a bridge for someone
Yet they do not meet you at the end
Do not fault them
What is important is your willingness to do for others
Without expecting anything in return
Don't ever lose that...

Aren't we all just recycled energy?
(Write a poem below)

SHEE

And maybe everything I have
I don't quite deserve

Like the smile upon your face
That is imprinted in my mind

Like the Sun that sets
And is always brave enough to rise

The rain as it falls
Washing away my woes

But I can assure you
That anything I have ever loved
Has been well cared for and protected

And I will use each breath I have left
To make myself worthy of you

Worthy for you
For you, my everything

IT'S ALWAYS BEEN YOU

The tone of your heartbeat
Lives within the warm walls of my soul
A sweet, melodic energy etched in my memory
It is true, some songs play endlessly
Stop and listen
I hear it
I hear you
Oh, how I hear us
The tone of magic embodied in a heartbeat

SHEE

August had come
All whirl, no wind
On that Monday
I thought I'd never see
In P.E. class
As we practiced our volleys
In my gym clothes
That smelled of last week
Slow and exhausted
And still recuperating
From my self-inflicted poisoning

I told my best friend
I had attempted to take my life
The words flowed in slow motion
Reluctant to experience release
Embarrassed to be heard
I don't know why I told her
At the time, I was so ashamed to be alive
To have lived to face yet another failure

One that would have ended my pain
Maybe I couldn't keep it a secret
And needed someone to tell
Maybe the burden was too heavy to hold
In my weakened, brittle state
And then, she just stared at me
With eyes unsure and sad
I felt a rush of panic, a pang of overwhelming regret
Say something!
Please say something!
I thought in my head
Until the coach blew the whistle
…

And she dropped the ball and hugged me tight
Holding me in hope
In a split second, I felt loved and wanted
Her silence was not what I wanted to hear
But her warmth was what I needed to feel

We never spoke about it
Our unspoken bond
That hug helped me want to live
Because, sometimes all we need is a hug
Not to fix us, but to hold us together

Sunpreet "Sunny" Bal
1985-2020

Dedicated to the Bal Family

March 5, 2020
Two days ago, one of my childhood best friends passed away. I wrote this poem about a year ago with the hope of reconnecting with her and sharing it. Over the years, we would serendipitously run into each other. We'd bump into each other at stores or nights out, and it felt like old times. Life just happens, and it's been around five years since I last heard her voice. Our last conversation was a brief phone call, discussing the possibility of having lunch. Sadly, it never came to pass.

Reflecting on eighth grade, I vividly remember everything that transpired that day. I recall more of that day than I can of the one I attempted to take my life. Prior to the day in P.E. when I awoke from my failed attempt, I had told myself I would try again. But she held me together with a single hug. Her power was profound. Now, I won't have…

the opportunity to share this with her, to express my gratitude or tell her how much I love her. I know I can't turn back time, and it may take a while to find closure in her untimely passing and the irony of our situations. All I can do is honor her while I'm still here.

Sunpreet "Sunny" Bal, always had a smile on her face. That gorgeous smile could be seen from miles away. Her eyes, so bright, the stars didn't stand a chance. She was full of love and life. She was kind, generous, and supportive to the ones she loved. There will never be another like her. She will live on in our hearts forever.

Sunny, my *jaan*, I know you're with me. How can you not be? When the Sun rises, when I see a pretty sunflower, or when I see our pictures together, I will say your name and smile. Till we meet again.

IT'S ALWAYS BEEN YOU

SHEE

Little brown boys
And little brown girls
With the names they can't pronounce
Do not come to America
America is not the dream
This place of evil and greed
The land of the free
Is a myth that sits on the very tip of Pinocchio's nose
Lies, dressed in promises
Deceit topped with cherries

Little brown boys
And little brown girls
With the hearts they lock in cages
Do not come to America
America is a farce
This place of confederate flags and white hoods
The land of opportunity
Is a fallacy even Aristotle could not decipher
Robbery, disguised as philanthropy
Culture through appropriation

Little brown boys
And little brown girls
The ones who go missing without media attention
Do not come to America
America is not a home
This place of stolen land
The land of wealth
Is a debauchery of materialism and classism
Thievery, impersonating discovery
Maps claiming legitimacy

…

Little brown boys
And little brown girls
The ones who look like my children
The ones who look like me
We need you in America
But the white man who sits in a white castle
Makes this place unsafe
He calls you illegals
Murderers and rapists
Conclusions, interpreted as inclusion
Prejudice camouflaged as morals

The Earth spins forward
Yet, America is so backwards
I am American
Yet, the color of my skin
Gives them the right to question my legality
Go back to where you came from
The lady whose skin is milkier than porcelain
Hisses to me
You don't belong here…
Then where is it I belong?
This place, America…
Where the roses smell of angst and uncertainty
The air of disappointment and grief
Where my brother, a dreamer
Is forced to limit his dreams

Little brown boys
And little brown girls
The ones who look like me
The ones who love like me
We want you in America
…

SHEE

The ones who know your worth
We will continue to fight for you
And pave a golden path
So you can find your way here
When it's safe for your American dream

What is your biggest regret?
Write it down. Accept it. Let it go.

SHEE

Sometimes, when it feels hard to love myself
I dress myself in song
With eyes shut
And hands, gently to my chest
I sing…

Low, and soft, so no one can hear it
A love song, a reminder
That I am, and have always been
Capable and worthy of love

Because I am,

Love.

IT'S ALWAYS BEEN YOU

You can't keep trying to save the world...
When you're barely above water
Tippy toed, neck deep
With little visibility

You see, these waters
The ones you use as an escape
To avoid tending to your own scars
Are always murky, always cloudy
The uncertainty
The unknown
The burden

How can you save anyone?
When you can't be sure you'll save yourself

Come in from the water
Onto solid ground
Save yourself first
Learn to sew up your wounds
Learn to swim in your own oceans
Learn to listen to your heart

Eerie candlelight
That playfully bounced off the shiny waxed wooden pews
The robust punch of frankincense
That forced me to pinch my nose
Hymns I could never understand
That Mommy made me sing
In the too tight polyester dress
That always made my eczema flair
At a church where I'm sure I never belonged
I never found the God that Mommy promised there was

In the bed of my abuser
Where my eyes were always shut tight
Where I prayed for Mommy to come to my rescue
In my five-year old little body
With the Elmo bandaid covered scraped knees
I never found the God that Mommy promised there was

In my bedroom
Where I laid awake most nights
Twirling my hair and wondering if my father missed me
While the big Jesus frame, Mama bought me
Lit my room a soft orange
In my bedsheets that were always too hot
But always ice cold
In a home where I always felt unseen and alone
I never found the God that Mama promised there was

Three decades and some years later
In the body that bore four beautiful humans
The one that grew gardens
Around the linings of invisible scars
With feet that have walked a million miles
…

And the eyes that have seen both Heaven and Earth
I finally found the God that Mama promised there was

SHEE

I hear it in the giggling children
Born of my womb
The whistling of the kettle
For six a.m. tea
The melodic snore
Of the man I've loved for twenty years
The exaggerated smacking
Of my mother's wet kiss
The passing of a train
In the midnight hour
The clickety-clack of my footsteps
As I follow my dreams
The slamming of doors
That were never meant to be opened
The pitter-patter of rain
On my windowsill
The lapping of waves
Playing tag with the shore
The scribbling of a pen
As I write away my troubles
The honking of cars
In Bay Area traffic
The closing of a book
That ended too soon

Can you hear it?
My life in sound…

IT'S ALWAYS BEEN YOU

In your mom's green car
The one you never asked to borrow
That always smelled like cinnamon
As we drove down Highway 17
Usually ten miles over the speed limit
We shared some of my cherished moments

There was always so much silence between us
But, I never cared
Grins, permanently affixed to our faces
Our hands always locked together
I always thought they fit so perfectly then
Even as the sweat laced our palms
We never dared let go

Our love, so young, so new
Warmed the car rides with sweet possibilities
Maybe we were both too afraid to speak
Fearing our happiness was only a dream

Now, silence sits heavily on our shoulders
As we sit, driving down new highways
In the car we bought on our own
Our hands to ourselves
When was the last time we held them?

Each of us with so much to say
But lacking the courage to say any of it
I know you hate my car freshener, but I leave it
Hoping you'll say something, anything
To break the ice, that has found it's home between us

And somehow,
This still feels like poetry
All of it
All of this...
Even the darkness

Glass lungs
Somehow tender and pained
From years of held breaths
Too afraid to be released
For a breath was not an escape
But a path to demise
A constant reminder of resilience
After all, breathing does not help flowers bloom
Or help the seed root
Or help the days stretch their muscles

No, not breathing
Or, at least not these lungs of mine
For these lungs
These lungs of tempered glass
And battle wounds
They breathe me closer to death
Each breath, a reminder that life is not guaranteed
And that death is the ultimate commitment

I'd be lying if I said breathing came easily
It's incredibly tough
Yet, it's all I have to give right now
And I'm making it enough

To all the flowers born in gutters
Darlings, you're beautiful too

I have tried my best to love others
In the way I know I should be loving myself
I light them up, *Shine baby, shine*
To combat darkness, and to help them grow
I give them my fractured bits
That are tired of holding on
In hopes of making them whole
And, in addition
Hoping it will somehow fill me up, too
But the soul knows
The Universe can only love you
As much as you love yourself

SHEE

        And when our children's children
        Must dig tunnels to find peace
        In a world never without fire
          It is you we will blame
            Yes, you
          You, the silent!

It's not true, you know
The whole notion that says,
You can't miss what you never had

They seem to forget about the dreams
The ones that tuck you in at night
The ones that end in a smile as you wake
The ones that give you chills
As you go on about your day

The scenarios that are created
Against the backdrop of a hopeful heart
So vivid, so real
You can feel the warmth of a tight embrace
That was never really there

Don't let them tell you
You can't miss what you never had
Because I am here
Missing what was never mine

SHEE

>She was a rare jewel
>In blinding fog
>And, she liked it like that

God planted a rose
Inside your Mommy's womb
And from that rose, you grew

Ten little fingers, and ten little toes
One radiant smile
And one dainty button nose

Twenty fleeting months
Six hundred thirty-three days
So many worlds, you did amaze

You will always be loved
Yaretzi, an Aztec name
Our hearts warmed, we'll never be the same

Yet, time shared is never enough
The strongest, happiest girl
Showed the world how to be tough

And even if we can't comprehend
God called you back home
No need to wander, no need to roam

You will always be loved
In our arms or worlds apart
Yaretzi, our girl, forever in our hearts

Yaretzi M.L.
2018-2020

Baby, we are the darkness
Our love is the light
(Don't let that shit go out…)

IT'S ALWAYS BEEN YOU

The words come out wrong,
Half-fast and exceedingly unsure
Almost as reluctant as they are scared
They don't seem to mean what I want them to
These words don't seem to be mine

They drip in thick sadness
Like sap seeking to escape the tree
Sadness is a feeling, but why is it my being?
The pen was my wand, creating imagery and blossoms
Amongst the ripening of daily inspiration
But it's not the same, not since you left

The words forsake me, the tone, distraught
Who got a hold of the pen, after I decided my path?
Who decided to write your exit?
After excitement glittered the hopeful trails of my heart
Because of the possibilities of a shared future

It hurts to write, and it hurts to breathe
Like my lungs are tempered glass
As the weight of loss sits piled high on my chest
Like unstable wavering bricks
Cracking me from the inside
Breaking more the already broken

Did you take the words with you?
Please tell me, for if I cannot have you here
The words, my words, if you've taken them
Well, at least you'll have a part of me
Even if I'm here missing you

SHEE

I lit two candles
One for each year of your life
And whispered your name
Once, twice, so many times
So, when it was time to leave
You'd follow the sound of your name
Into the light, and you'd find your way home
Oh, how you deserve to be home

I miss you…

He said he wanted to swim in the ocean
To feel the rush of the current
And the chill of the water
But we were miles from the shore
So, I cried him a river instead
Angry there were no waves, he walked away

Nothing is ever good enough, is it?

SHEE

Sometimes, I leave my heart a note
And tell her I'll return
Do not wait for me
But leave the light on
I'll be home soon

I pack my things and make the trek
To spend some time in my head
As I step inside, I can't help but see
How much she's let herself go

The windows and walls are veiled thick
With webs of self-doubt
The cabinets hang unhinged
From bearing the overwhelming weight of anxiety
And all the plants dangle limply
From the lack of watering and tenderness

I pause and sit on the floor
Unsure of where to begin
Part of me wants to escape back to my heart
Where I know I truly belong, but this is my home, too

So, I lock the doors and begin the task of tending
I start slowly and on my own terms
Pacing myself so I don't become overwhelmed

I sweep away the webs of doubt
Reinforce the cabinets to allow for more weight of angst
And I pot new plants capable of holding in more love

Hoping that the next time I come to stay
…

All will be well, requiring less care
Because as much as it hurts to come back to this place
After having found solace within my heart
I have no choice but to sometimes live inside my head

SHEE

I sat in her office
45-minute sessions
Two times a week
For almost a whole year
But I stopped going out of fear
Because I couldn't keep facing the truth
What are you so afraid of?
Why don't you want to let go?
She asked me
Like I didn't ask myself those same questions
Time and time again

The truth was I've always been an addict
Dependent on the thing that kills me inside
It's not a drug
Although it turns you ugly
Gives you mood swings
Sometimes even weight gain
It makes you hide under covers
Because you don't want to face the day
It makes you frown
Because smiling becomes too much work
You disassociate
Because it's easier than living

And as bad as all those things are
I still didn't want to let go of my Depression
I have lived so long with it
And even though its taken so much from me
I've always felt more with it, than without it
How could I let it go?
It's part of my identity
It's how I create
…

I'm too scared to part with it
Because at times in my life
It was the only thing I had
The only thing willing to hold me
And at those times it didn't let me go

Who would I be without it
I pleaded my case
She just stared at me
And I'd seen eyes like hers before
Concerned and sad
Contemplating what she would say
But the forty-five minutes were up
And it was my time to go
See you next week…
We will start where we are leaving off

But she never got that far
Because I never went back
So she never got the chance to wield her therapy sword
And take away what I know best in the world
And here I am
With Depression helping me write
Forcing my hand
To let everyone know it was not it
That told me not to go back
It was me, the woman with abandonment issues
Too afraid to show up for herself
And leave that next session alone
I'm sorry I can't let go

SHEE

>She wore stars in her eyes
> Rain in her heart
> And the Moon in her soul

IT'S ALWAYS BEEN YOU

Your lips, stained red
From all the cherries you ate
Like the juice tried to escape your **m**outh
But you were having none of that

Cherries, your f**a**vorite fruit
That tasted so much sweeter
Because you picked them **y**ourself
And I could do nothing else but stare and smile
As you gigg**l**ed with full, red, flustered cheeks
Almost as rosy as your stained, sticky fingers

I told myself, *Don't forget this mome**n**t*
Hold onto it, do not let time take it away

And here I am, years later, remembering that moment
How much pride you had,
In your tippy-toed cherry-picking skills

That moment, all the moments
That I hold so dear to my **h**eart
That I can remember just like yesterday
Make all the hard times worth it
It makes everything okay

You allow him to love you in the worst way
Maybe his love is a reflection
Of how you love yourself

No excuses, list 5 things (or more) that you absolutely love about yourself. The things that make you, you.

SHEE

And she said…
I still love you
But now, I love me more
I choose me
And you, you should choose you

There is growth in goodbye

IT'S ALWAYS BEEN YOU

Nobody taught me the proper way to miss another
They didn't tell me missing someone
Doesn't look like hours spent in the mirror
Telling yourself you're not good enough
Or scattered pictures on the floor
Trying to relive what you will never have again
(or maybe never had)
Or trying to create phantom embraces
That have long gone cold from years without

No, they didn't tell me
I had to learn it all on my own
I had to struggle through to find inner peace
But, maybe I can offer some guidance
So please, let me share with you
How missing another should look

Look in the mirror and affirm your self-worth
Place special photos in an album for safekeeping
(never throw them away)
Learn to embrace yourself in times of doubt
Disconnection doesn't diminish your self-worth
Wish them well and live a damn incredible life
And miss them from afar

SHEE

Oh, how she loves differently in the dark

Listen closely as you hear the birds serenade the Sun
And the way the wind dances
With the playful leaves in the trees
And the roar of the ocean
As it rushes to meet the sand on the lonely shores
And the way your heart chooses to beat
With so much love

Listen, you can hear hope

SHEE

> There was a time I loved fear
> More than I took the time to love, love
> I'm still learning that where there are thorns
> Doesn't always mean there are roses

IT'S ALWAYS BEEN YOU

She will pour herself into you
Every piece
Every fragment
Every breath
She will pour and pour
Even when you don't want her anymore
So, don't reciprocate in the beginning
And then shut yourself off
Because she is incapable of a limited love

All or nothing, Baby

SHEE

They walk right past me because I am not a rose
I do not bloom gracefully for the world to see
I am never chosen to adorn a bride's bouquet
And never plucked as a sweet memento of the day
No, I am a wildflower
I weather storms too tough for silky petals
And, when I am bored, I antagonize the heat
To wilt my ambition
It never will
I grow through cracked concrete
And alongside abandoned highways
I am fearless
Nothing I have gone through has made me soft
Quite the opposite, I can assure you

I am a wildflower.

sometimes, the soul will say, "let's reinvent ourself, shall we..." but the heart is never ready. you see, the heart is a skeptic, even if she is a fool. yet, she has no choice but to ride along on this journey because what good is a heart without a soul? the transformation will be difficult, sometimes excruciating, but trust the process. the soul belongs to the universe; it will take you places your heart is too afraid to go.

things you will discover after a rebirth...

- *you're both insecure and confident about this new person you've become*
- *the things that once fulfilled you no longer do*
- *you seek to fill your life with things that have meaning and purpose*
- *life feels surreal, so unfamiliar, different*
- *you want to spread your wings, see things you never seen, feel something you've never felt, experience big, deep, fulfilling moments*
- *you will start to question everything (life, love, faith...)*

cheers to loving this version of yourself
it wasn't easy, but baby, you made it

SHEE

> Look at how beautiful you are
> How you glow
> All dressed up in sunshine

IT'S ALWAYS BEEN YOU

Sometimes I like to sit alone outside
On a chilly winter day
And watch the clouds drift
Wherever they choose to wander
How they assume new forms
With each passing gust of wind
How they choose to be fearless in their purpose
And, move with bold, unapologetic grace

It always gets me thinking
Of my fortune and my pain
If I had a choice
Would I live this life again?
I start to imagine reliving this life
And, if I could rewrite it all
All the changes I would make
The heartache I would avoid
But, most of all
I think about you
If I made some changes and took alternate paths
Would you still find me?
And claim me as yours once more?

No easy road is worth taking
If it does not lead to love

Write a haiku with the word **heartbreak** below:

Kiss heartbreak with tongue
and, make love to disaster
no one has to know

Purpose lives on the dew drops
That glimmer upon a blooming flower
On the sunrise-lined hilltops
Of a brand new day
On the tip of a scribbling pencil
That is writing the dreamer's destiny

Purpose lives here
And it also lives there
Where, maybe, we can't touch
Or maybe, where we can't see
But, it's there, in the knowing
And, maybe, that's enough
Just knowing
That purpose lives…

Maybe I got so swept up in your love
No matter how bad it was
Because I was so tired
Tired of trying to figure out
How to love myself

And for that, I'm sorry
For putting all the pressure on you
But now that I think of it
We were both neglecting self-love
And in the process, we showed our affection
In passive-aggressive love
And resentment-filled I love you's

SHEE

I hold you close
And it is like cupping sunshine in my chest
Warmth
Love
Maybe there is no difference
You have always been mine
Haven't you?

And they give me a special day
To celebrate my title
But I would be nothing
Had you never called me home
Everything I have become
Everything I will be
Is because of you
My greatest love story
My happy beginning

All I want is to slow down
For time to hold my hand
Instead of always being ten steps ahead
For my heart to respect my chest
Instead of always building fires
For my eyes to open wider
Instead of looking for what they can't see
All I want is to slow down
To Slow...
Slow...
Slow

So thin is the veil of life
That maybe our true purpose
Comes after our last breath

To all the ones who left us too soon…

Self-loathing came for a visit today
She always has this way of sneaking up on me
Probably more so than others
Always around the same time too
It isn't like I can do much to stop her
When she visits, she finds comfort
By sitting atop my shoulders
She's always heavier than I remember
Like she's taken in more souls in her absence

I do my best to ignore her
But, one day I look in the mirror
Self-loathing just smiles
And I'm not even sure of who I'm looking at
Is that really me? Is this who I really am?
This sad version of a not-ever-so-happy woman
With sadness in her eyes
Is that really me?
I swear yesterday I smiled
That was yesterday, right?
I laughed too, I think
But, I'm not really sure, I'm never really sure

And, I never quite understand
Why happiness tends to be temporary figure in my life
Just like the father who gave me my name
So, I avoid mirrors
To avoid the disappointment that will look back at me
To avoid having to look myself in the eyes
Knowing that I promised I'd never come back to this place
To this unsafe space of self-loathing

SHEE

I was dead inside, long before you ever met me
Beaten up and bruised by all the odds stacked against me
Boldly broken and fiercely soft spoken
An acceptor of cruel losses
Knocked down on my knees
Bowing down to wooden crosses
- Shee, May '97

IT'S ALWAYS BEEN YOU

There are days I imagine running into you
In the midst of a chaotic day
Where, maybe I'm running errands
Or late for a very important appointment
I'd be frazzled, a literal mess
Ready to call it quits and head home
But then, out of the corner of my tired eyes
I would see you
You'd turn your head, seeing me too
We would lock eyes
Would we look away,
And act as though it never happened?
Would you run to me
Telling me how much you've missed me
Or, would it be me
Who runs to you, full of sobs and trembling hands?

I imagine every scenario
Even the ones where we walk away
Where the only thing we hear is our breaths
Livening up the stale air
I like that scenario best
No expectations
No awkward *hellos* or grim *goodbyes*
And as much as I know it will hurt
I hope it comes true
Even if it's only to walk away
Just one more time

SHEE

Shame followed me into womanhood
And for many years, I wore it like a heavy shawl
Something I knew had no purpose
But I didn't know how to throw out
I was too ashamed to accept pleasure from my husband
In the places where lovers touch
See, it was in those places
Where a predator had touched first
In those places, he had made feel profane
Made me wish for death
To be anyone, anything, but me

It wasn't fair, you know
To my husband, this man who worshipped me
Who worshipped not only my heart
But the misplaced body of ruins that came with it
Who wanted nothing more to receive the same affection
He so freely gave
But it took me years to open up, to share my body
And to unlock the doors of intimacy
That we both deserved to enter

Down that road of healing
It wasn't always easy
To climb the mountains of inner turmoil
Uncertainty, and fear
And to have to watch the man I love fight insecurity
Because the walls I had built were not only too high
But too thick
From the continuous years of applied self-doubt

But somehow, albeit slowly, the shame became strength
Where by allowing myself to be sensual
…

And to feel anything but shame
Is and was the biggest *fuck you* I could ever give
To that low life piece of shit
So, he can take the shame he gave me
Because, like him, it's worthless

SHEE

IT'S ALWAYS BEEN YOU

I touch my cheek
And I rub it softly
It is warm and soft
Like the warmth on a petal
On a warm spring day
Your love is still with me
The trace of your kiss
A touch of your soul
A lasting perfume
Of all that is good

SHEE

She's back
And this time
It feels like she's moving in for good
I hold the door open for her
As she moves in her belongings
She steps on my toes, purposely
Just to see if I budge
Her eyes, sharper than daggers
Cut deep into my soul
I try to find my voice
And tell her she isn't welcomed
But nothing escapes
It's as if my courage left
As soon as it saw sight of her
She's back
And this time
I'm not sure if I have any power left
Inside of me
To make her leave

Welcome back, Depression…

IT'S ALWAYS BEEN YOU

SHEE

You will make any excuse at first
Any reason to dismiss the true nature of their behavior
Maybe even blame yourself

But, the truth is
You don't deserve disaster
Just because it's dressed in possibility

You will learn, eventually
That choosing them over yourself
Will leave scars
Not just invisible ones
But visible ones too

The scars are always visible in the eyes
And, baby, your eyes say it's time to say goodbye

I drove past Hope
Alongside a forgotten highway
She was sitting there
Twiddling her thumbs
Without a care in the world

I reversed, rolled down my window
And examined her up and down
She was disheveled, dirty
And probably parched from the beating Sun

But she smiled, her eyes lighting up
As the smile reached her cheeks
Are you waiting for someone? I asked, happily

Her smile was contagious
Why, yes, she exclaimed,
YOU!

That's how I found Hope
Unexpectedly, but happily
And I've loved her ever since

SHEE

> Wake me from my slumber
> Kiss me in the rain
> Embrace me in this thunder
> Hold me close to ease the pain

If you met your five-year-old self, what would you do? What would you say? Write it down below.

IT'S ALWAYS BEEN YOU

It was so easy to get lost in you
The complexities of your love
Always made me curious
Intrigued, to say the least
Causing me to dig deeper and deeper
Into the possibilities
That were always laced in uncertainty
Maybe it was unfair of me
To put such a heavy burden on you
Expecting you to love me
When I didn't even love myself

SHEE

And you fought against me
Always resisting the love I so freely gave
Carrying me miles only to leave me stranded
Like a burden you had no choice but to bear

But, I made my way back to you
Always with arms wide open
Waiting for your cold embrace
Sometimes you would hold me
In what almost felt like love
But most likely only pity
I didn't care

I am characterized
As a patient woman
Always willing to wait
Maybe a bit stubborn
A tad overly naive
So every time you ran
Huffing and puffing
Just to get away
I chose to follow
So I could enlighten you
With the type of love
I knew you were capable of

It wasn't that you did it on purpose:
The pushing
The receding
The hiding
No, you were the sunshine behind the clouds
Wanting to give me the warmth
You knew I deserved

…

And even though
You kept the darkness you inherited alive
You also learned to tend and sow

Planting little seeds of hope
Here and there
Not knowing the roots grow first
Before the fruit
Look at how far you've come
Look at what you've created
What we have created
I believed in you
Darling, I still believe

So when you start the storms
No ship would ever dare sail
I put on my raincoat
Hold on tight, and smile

Baby, didn't you know?
I love the rain.

You hold the weight of it in your palm
I know you're afraid to let it go
For beauty is within it
Even if it can be so ugly
Even if it can destroy a soul
But we both know the lesson is in the pain
So, when you've learned it
And learned it well
Say farewell
Farewell pain

Farewell

See, there is a difference between you and I
One I'm sure you try to ignore
But, words—
These words—
These words I bleed
My words
They have saved me
Kept me alive
Helped me breathe
Helped my heart to beat

Yours are to prove a nonexistent point
Yours are to compete in a nonexistent competition
My words, invisibly tattooed on my skin
Will shine brighter than yours ever will
Yours, the ones you seek approval of
The ones you need others to read

But authenticity breeds resistance
You, you chase Sunshine
Not because you love the Sun
But because you can't stand to be in the dark
Me, I chase the Moon
Because I'm not afraid to face the light
Even if I live in the dark

Maybe the connection is disconnection
Once together, and now, not so
Maybe the communication is miscommunication
Something once heard and now, not so
Maybe we tried, and it wasn't good enough
Because you cannot accomplish something with a try
But only with the push of a do
Maybe you used my ears to belt off your woes
But never opened yours because you don't value mine
Maybe it hurts me, but you'll never know
That you open doors but lock them so I can't come in
Maybe it's your loss
Maybe it's mine

When I die
Tell them how much I loved them
Tell them how much I cared
But tell them I'm not taking them
With me after this life
They don't deserve the space there

SHEE

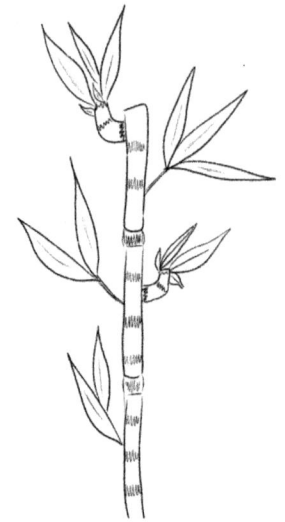

We spent the afternoon napping
Under the Sun and her (sun)flowers
Laughing and giggling
Giggling and laughing
Tracing our fingers through petals
Surely born of magical rays
Naming baby ones that hadn't yet
Found the power to bloom
Counting the rows of happiness
That would fade after Summer
And, I like to think
That maybe
Just maybe
Those lovely yellow flowers bloomed so bright just for us
A show only we had the privilege of witnessing
Under the Sun and her (sun) flowers

    Inspired by Rupi Kaur's, *The Sun and Her Flowers*

SHEE

As broken beings
We walk around believing in others
Who never believed in us in the first place
More than we believe in ourselves
Don't mistake loyalty for instinct

Trust your gut
It's your heart's best friend

I pulled at your shirt
Sobbing hot tears I'd hoped would melt your heart
Believe in me, I pleaded
More like a wish
In the tone of pathetic

Believe in yourself, you spat through gritted teeth
As you aggressively pulled away
Leaving me to drown in your words

But somehow
Those words were magic
The kind of magic you wish you never had
But grateful for at the same time

Because believing in myself
Only helped me to realize
I no longer believe in us

SHEE

Up a hill, and through the trees
Away from the bustling city
There is a graveyard of broken promises

On the nights when my heart feels the pull of sadness
I go to the garden and pluck sweet flowers
And make a modest bouquet
I make the journey in the dark, all on my own
There are no gravestones
But I know where your broken promises lie

As my footsteps approach
I hear them turning in their grave
I lay down next to the unmarked grave
And place the flowers atop the bed of grass
Decorated with dew

I spend the time singing sad love songs
Talking out loud on what could have been
If only you would had kept them instead
I remind them that I don't blame them for my pain
I blame myself for believing in what I couldn't see

On these nights, but always in the distance
I see your shadow
You never come too close

Instead, you watch me cry
As I perform solo rituals atop a jam-packed grave
You haunt me, *you haunt me still*
At the graveyard of broken promises

Our love lives within the echoes of disembodied voices
Some that sing, and some that scream
Suspended in mid air, afraid to move
What is the next move?
Unable to take flight, unable to touch solid ground
For fear lives there, and heartbreak fancies stepping on toes
There it stays stuck, unable, unwilling
To move back down to Earth
To frolic with consequence, to be brave and climb above
The thorn-filled barriers of hesitation
To reach what could truly be

Instead, our love stays suspended
While we crush our mutual dreams
The ones salted and shriveled from tears
As we turn our backs on each other
Instead of holding each other in warmth

We are fools, aren't we?

I saw the way the clouds kissed the Sun
As he made his way to bed
And I knew everything was going to be okay

The world stares, puzzled
As the words weep from my skin
I am still beautiful…
I am still beautiful…

Believing is seeing, right?

SHEE

On the summer nights
That live playfully
Laced in between the sweaty palms
Of soon-to-be lovers
The ones sticky
From eating sweet watermelon wedges
Chilled in the icebox
Right next to dad's beer
We found a bit of who we wanted to be
Stitched-together smiles
Foreign-like belly laughs
Requited love
As slow and fast
As the rhythm of a warm sorbet sunset
In a cotton candy drizzled sky
Where we still live on
Where our *baby* love still lives on
There are infinite infinities within our love
And I am living each one

Oh, those summer nights...

> Break through the dark clouds
> Shine on her, give her warmth
> *Mother Sun*, light her up

Write a haiku using the word **Sun** below:

SHEE

I've always felt the need to defend who I am
Or why I move the way I do
Why my smile is just a wee bit crooked
Or how I laugh deep within my belly

I never said I was all good, I admit there is a darkness
That wiggles its way through my veins
Darkness needs a home too

I never said I had it all figured out
I've lost my way so many times
I've lost count

This life is a labyrinth
I love a challenge

What I am saying is these pieces of me
The ones that I so visibly bleed, they are mine

You do your best to overshadow all that I have built
And just because the shutters are a tad unhinged
Believe me when I say
The foundation is more robust than any gust of wind
Than any terrifying storm
Or any beast impersonating an angel

No more defending who I am
No more explaining
I am who I am
Someone you'll never be

IT'S ALWAYS BEEN YOU

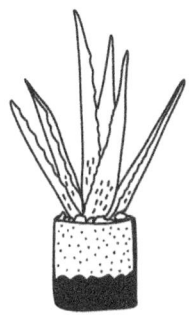

SHEE

I feel you
And I'm trying not to give
You the attention that you crave
But, I'm tired
I'm tired of being tired
And, I'm tired of always finding
My way back to you

Just when I see the rays of sunshine
On the petals of a flower
Or when the satisfaction I feel from
Sipping a cup of coffee
Is more intense than yesterday
When I hear my favorite song
Like it is playing just for me

Why?
Why do I slip back to you
Like a weed desperate for attention?
Why do you hold me so tight
I can't help but succumb to your embrace?

Even if the world was mine
I'm sure you'd find a way
To take that from me too

These are the days I feel my weakest
These are the days I wish I had someone…
Anyone
To cry my grievances to

These are the days I wish I knew
How to scream a deafening scream
…

So I didn't have to hear my thoughts
Losing once again to you

These are the days I wish
I could ignore whatever it is you do to me
Whatever power you have over me
Whatever this, whatever is

Leave me alone!
Wait.
No.
Wait.
Yes.

If everything and everyone
Is so good at leaving me
Then why, Sadness
Do you find the need
To stick around and watch me bleed?

SHEE

> Stop telling me to hold on
> When clearly, you've already let go

And sometimes I ask
What gives you the right,
To take up so much space in my life?
Who gave you a key to this home?

Yes, GRIEF, I'm speaking to you…

SHEE

I know how it may seem
That I am so unwilling
So incapable of truly loving myself
But, I do
Somewhere in this ever-mending heart
Lies a hidden pocket of peace
That is so filled with self-love and adoration
It bulges at the seams
I keep it tucked away, deep within
Like a secret I'm not willing to share
To keep it safe for when I need it most

I know how it may seem
I know it may seem obvious
But, you're wrong
Even if it's hard to see
(Self)love lives here too…

We are the same person,
We are the same, Honey…
So, and if he was right—
We both loved each other so much
But what we both lacked
Was the ability to show it
The way we both needed to be shown

A Eulogy

SHEE

After you touched it
I didn't learn to love it
I despised it, purged it, starved it, wounded it
Tried to take the life from it, I cursed myself
I won't lie, I even cursed God, asking, "Why, why, me?"
It took decades for me not to feel
Your phantom snake-like fingers lingering on my skin
Even so, every now and again
I still feel you haunting me in my dreams

After you touched it, I didn't learn to love it
This body of a Mother
Who bore and birthed beautiful babies
Of a wife whose husband tried his best to help heal
The wounds you left behind
Even then, I could not learn to love it
Even then, I felt it okay to let it go
This body, the only one I've got
The one that holds the eyes
That cry seeing her children grow
The one that holds the broken heart
That still has the courage to beat
The one whose hands hold hope like it is a rare jewel

After you touched it, I never learned to love it
I never tried
But, there's always a start to each end

I'm learning...

In my dreams
We were always more
But dreams are lies
False promises to a hopeful heart
So, I dreamt a little less

Darling,

Your value does not come from who likes you - or who doesn't. Remember, not everyone appreciates fine wine.

Longing for love and abundance
From the clouds, a glimpse of heaven
Thoughts that whisper to her heart to come home
In an unfamiliar silent place
The color of the sea beneath the golden sky
Very fragile remnants
The tenderest sympathy
Her daring soul
She could believe
To find she was so perfectly alone

It's magic, you know?
That despite it all
You still learned to love

The most beautiful thing
The sweetest memories
Bright hopes, she wondered if she was dreaming
She didn't press her luck
Bidding farewell to the warm, merry day
Her eyes gleamed
To let go with heart
Mementos of lives lived
There seemed no more to say
By the light of the moon
The first step in a journey
Magic in truth
From sunrise till the shadows grew

And somehow, she's stitched together
With fire and ice
Gold and coal
Some things ugly
And some things nice

Close the door on once
Say goodbye to a forever
Revel in what is

Write a haiku using the word ***goodbye*** below:

SHEE

I always thought purpose came from
Finding myself in others
Some would say I cared too much
About who they thought I was
I spent so much of my life
Trying to mold myself
Into who I thought others wanted me to be
Instead of figuring out who I was
Now I know, purpose comes from finding who I am
Even when no one else cares to find out

Today I wrote you a letter
In the form of a dainty, unassuming poem
With trembling hands and an eager, misunderstood heart
I set it down next to your pillow
Where you slept peacefully, unaware

And there, that letter sat
Written in my handwriting
Using my favorite pen
On the pretty floral stationary
You bought me for my birthday

Waiting to be read
Waiting to deliver a message
Hoping you would read between the lines
Hoping you could decipher the call for help

I'll get to it when I have the chance, you'll say
Not knowing there is a fuse that has been lit
Words scrambling on paper, ready to detonate
Only to be diffused with understanding and patience

You will question why I could not tell you
That my heart pulses pain
Why I cannot see all of my blessings
Or why I am ready to rest beyond the dark

Why?

Because the words flow easier on paper
Then they ever have from these lips

SHEE

If the words choose to rip me open
I will give them their way
Let them slit my wrists with the pen
To use my blood as ink

And, when they are done
Even if it hurts
I will use those words
And the pain they unearth
To learn the lessons
And write my life

I sat hoping to be gifted it from the Moon
Or inherit its warmth from the Sun
See, I had always wanted love
I just never knew
I was love to begin with

Let heartbreak show you the way...

It's sad when you see a change in people; when their hearts go hard, and their eyes grow dark—especially when before they were so bubbly and light. Don't be fooled— heartbreak isn't meant to make you harder. It isn't meant for you to close yourself off or to leave behind people who have only wanted good for you. Heartbreak is supposed to show you exactly how you shouldn't love. It is supposed to...Well, you decide. Sooner or later, you'll realize it -- all in due time. We all have to learn the lessons in our own time.

SHEE

The little girl cries as she swims towards her pastor
She is about to embark on a journey, a mission
A commitment
Watching her in the community pool
Her church rented for the afternoon
As the Sun sparkles off the clear blue water
It takes me back a few years ago
When I gave my life to God
I remember quivering in the water
My cousin's hand on the back of my neck
Tears streaming down
The dip, the moment of becoming one with the water
As I confirmed my faith in God
The sense of community as the congregation
Roared with applause

Soon after that day
The lead pastor preached about God's disdain
For gays, premarital sex, his pro-hate views
And it made me feel small
For I cannot imagine a God
Who puts stipulations on what love should look like
A God that will send you to hell for loving to feel good
And a God that wants to separate us
Instead of bringing us together
I wanted to scream to the little girl
God will love you anyway
Swim away
God will still love you

But she cried happy tears
And even as she rose back above the water
I knew she would be okay
…

Because God will love her anyway
But I hope she grows to love everyone
And not just the people religion says are okay
Because God loves us anyway

August 19, 2019
Journal entry 231 of 365

Not too long ago, I was baptized as a Christian, and it was a beautiful experience. The connection I felt with God was surreal. However, shortly after my baptism, my nondenominational congregation began displaying warning signs. The lead pastor started discussing politics and his preferred presidential candidate, advocating that we distance ourselves from those who engage in premarital sex or those who choose to love individuals of the same sex, or other genders he considered "non-God made." I was appalled and deeply disappointed.

I have since moved away from organized religion and adopted a more spiritual perspective. No one should ever dictate how I or anyone else should worship or believe. I will never impose my beliefs on others either. Whether someone identifies as Christian, Catholic, Atheist, Hindu, Buddhist, Muslim, or follows any other belief, I respect and love them. In my eyes, we are all human beings trying to find our way, and there is no room for hate in my life. If someone preaches hate, division, or exclusion, we will never see eye to eye. I hold the value of respecting others in high regard. Love is love, and there is no place for hate within it.

SHEE

>   Of all the fleeting forevers
>   I may have in this lifetime
>   I hope the one we share is the longest

IT'S ALWAYS BEEN YOU

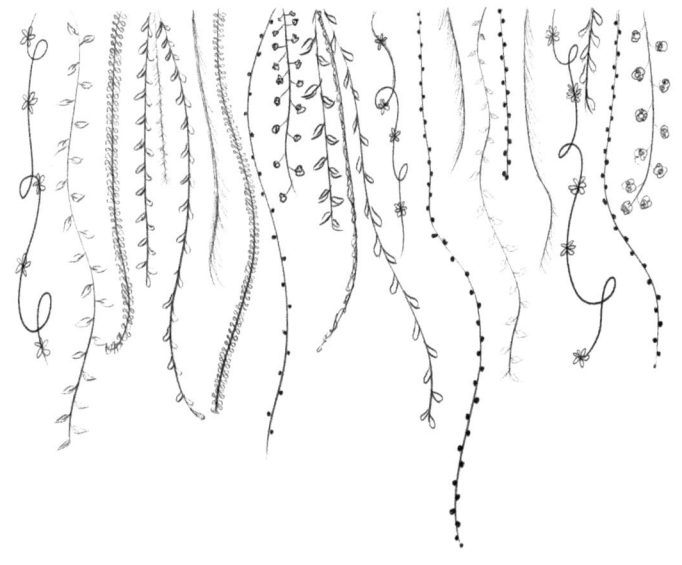

Leave me tomorrow
But today, I beg…
Lie and tell me you love me

I'll be brave tomorrow, I promise

SHEE

Deep within the fragile tendrils of my heart
You will find the story of my life
There you will find seasons of blooming
Barefoot dancing in the rain and Sun-kissed caramel skin
Girl talk with wildflowers
Laughter beneath playful willow trees

Burnt marshmallows, that I gladly ate anyway
Pages and pages, of books that taught me how to dream
Lullabies and love songs
That helped me go to sleep
But, to bloom was never easy

Destruction comes in many forms
Like the hand of a man, who touched wasn't his
Or the whisper, of a thought that tells you to end it all
Even the bitter silence
From the man who helped give you life

The truth is, I've died more times than I can count
For me, destruction is a wage I pay
Time and time again
To live, to breathe, to bloom
To feel anything at all

So, when I bloom, I **BLOOM**
But, who would've guessed
The price to live would be to die
And, I've gotten quite good at it

To die for a living

IT'S ALWAYS BEEN YOU

What we have is history
What we had is there
And no amount of future
Can ever take us back

SHEE

I promise you, there is bliss to be found in the storm

The hate I have for you
Long surpasses any love I have for you
Yet, even so—
You could never love me
Nearly as much as I love you

Everyone is special
Cheers to the ones who believe it
Make me a believer

IT'S ALWAYS BEEN YOU

The flower never questions
If it's wanted by the bee
Yet, here I've been my entire life
Questioning my worth
But maybe the question I should've been asking
Is if the people I love (and have loved)
Were good enough for me

SHEE

You will not always feel the light
And, you may not always see it
But, I promise
The light will always find its way back to you
What is yours will always be

Between this space of intimacy and time
This sacred place of vulnerability and prose
Here you are…

It's always been you

more from shee

You can find the following pieces in Shee's first collection:
If You Cannot Find Her, 2019.

I want to love, Love
>   Like the Sun wants to rise
>   And the Moon wants to shine
>   Like a flower wants to bloom
>   And the wind wants to blow

I want to love, Love
>   Even when the Sun cannot be warmth
>   Or when the Moon seeks to hide
>   Even when a flower loses her petals
>   Or when the wind needs its rest

I will love, Love.
>   In all ways
>   *Always*

If you see Sadness in my eyes
> Please do not attempt to remove what clearly belongs
> The Moon, with all its grandeur and genius
> Already tried to lift away the weary ghosts
> Who have found solace behind these lids to no avail

So, I sit back and wait longingly for the days
> That sadness will become filled with boredom
> It will leave to play in the rain
> But we all know the Sun
> Will come back to glitter the sky
> And Sadness will race its way back again
> To my dark brown eyes
> Because only darkness will do

If you see Sadness in my eyes
> Know Sadness doesn't live here
> It comes and goes as it pleases
> And, I haven't the heart to keep these eyes closed
> Because even Sadness needs
> A place to rest it's weary head

Sadness needs love too

If all that I have written
    Is evidence of a broken heart
    Then I shall enlighten you

In between these thighs
    The ones that rub together
    The ones I am too insecure
    To let the Sun see

In between these two thighs
    You will find the ruins of war
    One I didn't win
    But one I was never supposed to fight

MORE FROM SHEE

I have a secret
One I'm too ashamed to share
Even if you don't deserve
To share this life with me
There are spaces in this heart
In which I leave vacant just for you
The days where I am weak
And all too forgiving
I light a floral path for you
So maybe
If you feel you need me
You can find your way
And rest your head upon the soft spots
That haven't yet hardened to stone
You don't deserve the soft spots
But I save them just for you

When you think of me
I hope it feels
Like a whisper in a dark room
An icy chill
That crawls up your spine
A scare that scars you
Long after your first encounter
I hope you realize
That I'm no longer waiting
No longer on your time
But I will continue to haunt you
Even from afar

And,
> I had given you so much of me
> It was only in you
> Where I saw glimpses
> Of who I used to be

And,
> I hated you for accepting it all
> Knowing I would never say no
> To feel needed
> Was my kryptonite

And,
> Now she will never be mine
> That girl who needed
> But gave it all instead

And,
> Maybe that was my purpose
> I'm all used up
> There is no more
> No more to give

When I say
I am not the one
It is because once
I was the one who wrestled demons
While everyone watched me struggle
I was the one who cried whole oceans
While holding up mountains
So others wouldn't drown
I was the one who came back
From the edge of a crumbling cliff
To find solid ground for others to walk on
So, when I say
I am not the one
Believe me
I will no longer put myself
In situations that rip me to pieces
While others stay whole

MORE FROM SHEE

I don't do easy
Look at the disaster that is my past
The evidence all there
I continue to do things the hard way
But if my history has taught me anything
It is, easy does not build resilience
Easy does not give you tough skin
Easy does not make you smarter
And it certainly doesn't
Make you love harder

Sometimes we tell ourselves that
What we are missing is closure
Like the closure will sew up our wounds
And they will never be tender again
Don't be mistaken
Closure hurts too

MORE FROM SHEE

Last night I dreamt you loved me
But to remember is a force
Never dormant for too long
Woken by salty tears
And a revelation that dreams
Are sometimes lies dressed in hopes
I realized
No amount of love
Could make up for the amount of pain you caused
Last night I dreamt you loved me
But, I don't want that anymore

I didn't mean to be war
I tried to be the peace you wanted
But how did you expect me
To sit and choose silence
When you fought against me
Not for me

MORE FROM SHEE

We were young
Living for the days
We could escape to dance
In the mustard flower fields
Behind our broken home
Our clothes stained yellow
From rolling around
Those innocent blooms
Now, every time I see
Those lovely yellow petals
It brings me back
To when unassuming little flowers
Had the power to keep us from falling
When everything else in our lives was crumbling
I'm sure they didn't mind holding us up
Even if it was only
A few millimeters off the ground
Embracing our rowdy
So we didn't hit the dirt
Even if that's where
Life said we belonged

about the author

Shee is a Filipina American poet and writer, currently living in the Bay Area of California. Her interests include history, writing, reading, traveling, photography, and spending time with her family. This is her second collection of poetry.

facebook.com/shee_poetry
twitter.com/shee_poetry
instagram.com/shees_spirit
tiktok.com/@shee_poetry

www.ingramcontent.com/pod-product-compliance
Lightning Source LLC
Chambersburg PA
CBHW042322090526
44585CB00025BA/2809